# Cell Phones at School: Yes or No?

**by Mrs. Morrison's class**
**with Tony Stead**

capstone®
classroom

In today's classrooms, there is a growth in the number of students with their own cell phones. Cell phones can be used for a variety of purposes—but should they? That is the question that we intend to answer.

In our classroom, we have many students on both sides of this debate. Many think that cell phones should be considered for use in the classroom. Others disagree. They believe the negative consequences are greater than the benefits. You will be reading several statements for and against the use of cell phones in school. Once you have considered both sides of the issue, you will be able to choose which side has the stronger argument.

# Why Students Should Have Cell Phones

## by Oshai

Cell phones have many cool features like games, funny or scary videos, pictures, and many endless things you can do at home. From my personal experience, I would recommend that kids be able to use cell phones for nonstop education at school. It's important for kids to have phones in school for three specific reasons: research, education, and emergencies.

If children were to bring phones to school, they could have Internet access to the things most important in school. Consequently, the schools would not have to worry about trying to sustain the computer labs. All the other computers can be put to use by the children that don't have electronic devices. For example, I was able to use my phone to research a topic when all the other children were using computers. Because of that extra educational time, many positive things happened. Not only did I get to research this topic on my phone, but with that useful bit of time I also finished my project. With phones in the classroom, students will become more knowledgeable.

Cell phones are also useful if we need to contact parents for emergencies. Think about this: What if students weren't allowed to bring phones to school and a major emergency occurred? Even though teachers have classroom phones, they would not be as good as cell phones. Students would need to wait in line to talk on the phone. Classroom phones aren't as convenient or as safe as cell phones.

Smarter, safer, and more access to the Internet—that seems pretty convincing to me! Why would you NOT have cell phones at school?

# Cell Phones at School? It Just Shouldn't Be

## by Maddie

Ring! Ring! Clickety, click! This is what you would hear as people get phone calls and texts at school. There is nothing wrong with texting, calling people, and spending time on your phone—just not at school. Phones are a huge distraction, they can get stolen, and they are bad for your mental and physical health.

Cell phones distract and annoy many people, such as teachers, students, visitors, and other staff members. So not only do you get a bad grade, everyone else does too. By not having your phone at school, you are helping yourself and you are helping other people as well.

Another reason that cell phones are bad at school is that they can be stolen. At my old school, one girl had her iPad stolen. She was miserable for a while because of it. No one wants to be the person whose phone or device is stolen, but it can happen to anyone. It's better to leave expensive items at home.

Last but not least, a cell phone can cause bad eyesight, loss of patience, and loss of attention span. Many kids in our elementary schools already have cell phones, and they have difficulty paying attention because of them. Even adults struggle!

Are you convinced that cell phones don't belong at school? Leaving your phone at home gives you more attention and better eyesight, keeps your phone safe from theft, and helps you keep annoyances and distractions to a minimum.

# Cell Phones: Just Say No!

## by Elijah

I believe we shouldn't bring cell phones to school because they distract from classwork. In fact, there's nothing about them that's NOT distracting!

The ring of a cell phone distracts other students and teachers. Texting distracts the kids around the person who is texting. When kids have cell phones out they might be playing games instead of doing schoolwork or research. Cell phones could even lead to cyberbullying by text message or calls.

Theft is another huge problem with cell phones. You might leave your cell phone somewhere it could get stolen. A cell phone is tempting to a thief. According to one source, 1.6 million cell phones are stolen every year. In San Francisco 50 percent of all thefts are mobile devices.

Think about the facts. Do you want to keep distractions down? Do you want to be sure there aren't targets for thieves in your school? Do you want to prevent cyberbullying? If you answered yes to any of these questions, then you understand why it's important to keep cell phones out of school.

# No Phones at School

## by Laird

Bringing phones to school is a bad idea. Phones can be broken, stolen, lost, and used for bad purposes. These reasons should convince you: Leave phones at home!

Phones can get broken. They are expensive. If your phone breaks, your parents will most likely be mad. You can spill water on a phone or drop it, or a friend could accidentally break it. Imagine you're on the playground. You drop the phone, and someone steps on it. It's an accident, but the results are the same whether it was an accident or on purpose. Your phone is broken.

You bring a phone to school expecting that it will be safe and others will respect your property, but someone might be tempted to take it. If you drop it somewhere, another student might not know whose it is to return it. Taking a cell phone to school is definitely a great way to lose it forever!

Students may claim that they are doing research with their phones at school, but they might be playing games. They could be watching videos that aren't appropriate for school. Research is a great purpose for a phone, but calling and texting your friends at school is not.

Phones can be broken, stolen, lost, and used for activities that aren't appropriate for school. For those reasons, cell phones are best left at home.

# Why Kids Should Be Allowed to Bring Cell Phones

## by Taylor

Have you noticed that many students have phones? Should they leave these phones at home? No! There are good reasons to bring cell phones to school.

The first reason for allowing kids to bring cell phones to school is safety. Lots of schools are allowing kids to bring cell phones to school. One school district in Illinois is allowing kids to bring cell phones to help keep them safe. District representative Dan Domench stated, "Security and red alerts on terrorism became an issue." Consequently, cell phones can keep students safer by allowing them to communicate during an emergency.

Another reason cell phones are school-appropriate is that phones have educational things on them like math and reading apps. Teachers should check to see what students are doing on their phones and have time limits, but if students need to do research, a phone is a great resource.

Finally, when my class tried an experiment on cell phone use, the results were very positive. We learned to be responsible with our phones and to use them for research and reading. Students admitted to using phones 73 percent of the time for educational purposes only. We did a lot of research!

Now that you know my point of view, I hope that you will see phones aren't always a distraction for students. They can be used for many positive things!

# Why Cell Phones SHOULD Be Allowed at School

## by Ixtli

Cell phones—they are basically life in a little box with a screen. Everybody keeps debating whether kids should bring cell phones to school. Some people say that cell phones in school lower test scores and distract students, but cell phones are actually a lot of help.

First of all, communication is very important. Let's say it started snowing and the weather was bad enough that school was dismissing early. A long line of students could form as everyone tried to call home. It would be useful if you had your phone to call your parents. You forgot your homework? No problem! You left your backpack at home? No problem! You have your phone right there!

Cell phones can be used for research. Our school has a computer lab, but there aren't enough computers for everyone to research at once. You have to go to the lab and log in. It's just more comfortable researching on a phone. You can take it anywhere! A cell phone is portable. That makes it much easier to use than a computer, especially at your desk.

You could do so much with a cell phone. They are called "smart phones" for a reason. I personally think that we kids can handle having a cell phone at school. Maybe they should even provide them for us.

# Why We Should Have Our Phones

## by Mia

Should we have phones at school? I choose yes! Having a phone at school would help me learn more.

Cell phones are useful for projects. Imagine going to the computer lab and finding that all the computers are being used. You and your classmates can simply pull out your cell phones and search to find what you need. You'll be finished on time! If students are careful about their cell phone use, they're good to go—a world of research is right at their fingertips.

Reading is also something that is easier with a cell phone. At DEAR (Drop Everything and Read) time, you can read a book on your electronic device. When my class starts a novel study, for example, we can choose to read it as an e-book on our phones. Cell phones are great for reading during free time. Quiet reading on a cell phone won't disturb classmates. You can even use your phone to read to a buddy.

You can read on your E Books.

In addition to projects and reading, you can listen to music when you are doing individual work. For instance, you can listen while you are reading and while you are waiting in line for the teacher. Listening to music can help you pay attention and focus more closely on your work so that you are not distracted by what is going on around you.

These three reasons are just some of the ways that we can use phones to help us with our learning. What other ways do you think cell phones are useful for students? We'll find out if we can bring them to school!

# Should Students Be Able to Use Cell Phones in School?

## by Hannah

Parents, students, and teachers ask themselves this question every day. Should students be able to use cell phones in school? Yes, in my opinion, they should! Why do I think so? There are important reasons to allow cell phones at school.

Students should be able to use phones because they can use them for research. At our school, computer lab crowding is a real problem. Cell phones solve that problem.

In addition to being useful for research, phones are important for safety. What if there was an emergency and the teacher was not able to get to a phone? If the students had their phones, someone could call for help in a lockdown or a fire. The teacher may have a classroom phone, but it's good to have a backup, and there may not always be time.

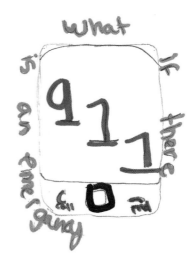

Some phones have inappropriate games, pictures, and music, but the teacher can set the limit on what students can and can't do on their phones. Some teachers might let students play games and take pictures if there was free time and work was done, but think of all the tests you could pass more easily having a cell phone for research and homework!

Most students can handle phones in school, and many people think it's a good idea to bring them there. I'm a believer.

# Cell Phones in School

## by Gwen

Cell phones are great devices for kids, so kids should bring them to school.

One reason for bringing phones to school is that phones are handy for reading. For example, if you forgot your novel and it's on your phone, you can use the electronic version. Or if you want to read a book to your reading buddy, you can just use the device. On a phone or tablet, you can download books and carry several of them at once.

Aside from reading, cell phones could make schools safer. Imagine that bad weather is coming and many students need to call home for rides. The line for the classroom phone is really long, so some students will be waiting a long time just to call home, not to mention how long the wait will be for parents once the calls are made. But if students can use their own phones, they can all call at once and get home safely.

Lastly, what if students need to do research and all the computers are taken? One time, all the computers in the lab were in use, so our teacher decided that we could use our phones. I learned a lot that day. In fact, I think that using cell phones could raise grades and test scores!

There are exciting reasons to have cell phones in school. They could help our grades, keep us safe, and allow us to read without having to carry around books.

# I Say No to Bringing Phones to School!

## by Lisette

Phones are great for using apps, going on the Internet, texting, and calling. But should students have these devices at school? Even though phones are very useful, I don't think they belong at school.

First of all, you could lose your phone at school. With so many students, teachers, and visitors, it's easy for someone to just pick up the wrong phone. Some students may be tempted to take a phone from another student. Teachers are too busy to lock up phones. It's just a big risk to have a phone at school.

Although phones can help keep people safe in emergencies, there are dangers to having phones too. If a student receives a strange text or call at school, he or she may not know what to do about it. At home, parents and family members can guide kids when they are unsure. But at school, it might be harder to get help and could leave a kid in a bad situation.

Proper writing and grammar by young people will become worse with cell phone use. According to a major education website, allowing students to bring cell phones to school will "exacerbate poor writing and grammar skills." Kids are getting extremely used to texting because it is a part of having a phone. Students have become dependent on the autocorrect feature of phones and electronic devices. Because of this, spelling and grammar skills are decreasing and students are getting lower grades. In texts between friends, kids are always shortening words and this is also showing up in the classroom writing.

Kids should not be able to bring phones to school because they may get lost or stolen. Phones are also a safety issue and can affect grades. These reasons should convince you that to keep our schools educational, cell phones should stay at home or securely tucked into backpacks.

# Why We Shouldn't Bring Cell Phones to School

## by Natalie

There are many reasons not to bring cell phones to school, but three important reasons are enough to convince me!

One reason for not bringing cell phones to school is to keep your messages private. If you have a phone at school, a friend could get into your text messages and text a friend of yours with something like, "Hey, we are never going to be friends again!" Passwords can prevent this from happening, but it's one of the risks of having a phone at school. You can peek over someone's shoulder and see something that should be private. That could lead to a lot of problems.

Cell phones also can distract kids from their work. Phones have movies, music, games, apps—all sorts of things competing for our attention. If students get lost in these activities, they can get into trouble and their grades could drop. Cell phones are just too distracting.

Finally, cell phones are small and easy to lose. It would be a huge waste of money to bring a phone to school and then never be able to find it again.

For these reasons, I'm keeping my phone safe at home instead of taking it to school.

# Say No to Cell Phones in School!

## by Lucinda

I know many kids wish to bring their phones and other electronics to school. However, there are many reasons why cell phones are still not allowed in most schools. And they are good reasons!

First of all, even though phones can be used for research, some kids may try to go on a site that they don't know is dangerous. They might give away personal information. Sometimes giving away unneeded information can lead to crimes.

Theft is a crime that can happen when a phone is brought to school. If a student accidentally leaves a phone in a desk, someone can steal it. Then the student with the stolen phone can't reach his or her parents or have access to research, books, or the Internet on the phone.

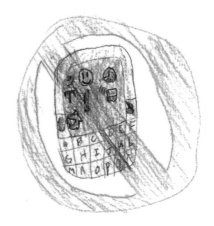

Last but not least, cell phones could make it look as if students are cheating. As we all know, most tests are to see where you are in a subject. Most of the time, a test is independent work and you can't use help. A student caught with a phone might fail as a result of the teacher thinking that the student was cheating by looking up the answers on a phone. Therefore the student might even fail the class.

These reasons explain my thinking about why students should NOT be allowed to bring phones to school. I hope you agree.

# No! No! No Phones!

## by Elek

A lot of people think that it is a good idea to bring a phone to school. But I think cell phones in school are a bad idea. You shouldn't be allowed to have them in school.

First, if you bring your phone to school, people will get distracted. You might be playing a game or searching for something that you are not supposed to. Someone else might be texting another student in class instead of listening. In both cases, students who are distracted do not know what to do.

What if you lose your phone or someone takes it? It is too big of a risk to bring your phone to school. Imagine your parents getting so mad! Then you cannot bring your phone to school—because you don't have one. If bringing your phone to school is that big of a risk, what is the point in bringing it to your school?

I think that it is not a good idea to bring a phone because they already have Nooks and computers. Plus, phones have slow Internet and content that is not appropriate for school. One time, I saw a student watching an inappropriate video while she was supposed to be researching conflicts.

Those are only three reasons why I think phones should not be at school. There are many more reasons, but that's just my opinion. Now you decide.

# Phones should be allowed because they ...

- have Internet access.
- can be used for research.
- allow contact with parents.
- keep people safe and secure.
- include educational apps.
- teach responsibility.
- help people communicate.
- are portable.
- keep kids from having to wait for technology.
- include e-books.
- have music that helps people focus on work.

# Phones should not be allowed because they ...

- can be a distraction.
- can be lost or stolen.
- can cause bad eyesight.
- could lead to bullying.
- can break.
- may include inappropriate content.
- could have inappropriate uses.
- cause poor writing and grammar skills.
- could lead to cheating.

The issue of students having phones in school and in the classroom is being considered more and more by parents, teachers, and school staff. Now that you have heard all of our reasons for and against the use of cell phones in school, what do you think? Use the arguments, and decide for yourself!

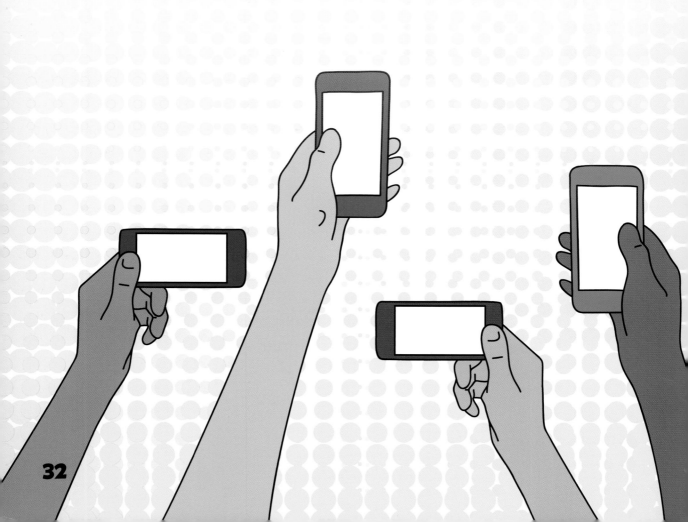